All About Goldfish As Pets

BY KAY COOPER

PHOTOGRAPHS BY
ALVIN E. STAFFAN

All About Goldfish As Pets

Julian Messner   New York

Published by Julian Messner, a Division of Simon & Schuster, Inc.
A Gulf + Western Company
1 West 39 Street, New York, N.Y. 10018. All rights reserved.

Printed in the United States of America

Design by Joseph J. Sinclair

Library of Congress Cataloging in Publication Data

Cooper, Kay.
   All about goldfish as pets.

   SUMMARY: An introduction to the selection, care, and breeding
of goldfish.
   1. Goldfish -— Juvenile literature. [1. Goldfish]
I. Staffan, Alvin E., 1924-   II. Title.
SF458.G6C66   639'.375'3   76-26519
ISBN 0-671-32801-8

**FOR MY CHILDREN,
ANN AND SUSIE
— WITH LOVE AND JOY!**

ACKNOWLEDGMENT

The author acknowledges the kind assistance of
Roger and Kris Tipps of Springfield, Illinois,
owners of an aquarium store.

Messner Books by Kay Cooper and Alvin E. Staffan

ALL ABOUT GOLDFISH AS PETS

ALL ABOUT RABBITS AS PETS

A CHIPMUNK'S INSIDE-OUTSIDE WORLD

Contents

Calico Pompon

Golden Fish

Fringetail

Bubble Eye

Fish with poppy eyes, fish with pompons, and fish with heads shaped like strawberries are fascinating. And they are all goldfish. But they are not always gold. They come in colors like red and blue and black, too. Some are two inches (5 cm) long. Others grow almost twenty-four inches (60 cm) long.

The goldfish's scientific name is *Carassius auratus*. *Auratus* is the Latin word for golden, and *Carassius* is the scientific name for the crucian carp. Goldfish belong to the carp family. Carp are brown and light-green fish. They are used as food and are found in parts of the United States, Asia, Europe, and Australia.

A thousand years ago, the Chinese found golden carp swimming in streams. These fish were so beautiful that they were kept alive as pets in ponds and clay bowls. The Chinese even made earrings for them. Colored stones were strung on tiny golden loops, which were slipped through the openings on the heads of the fish.

Many Chinese and European folktales are told about goldfish. A Hungarian story tells about a prince who loved fish and fish ponds. He traveled to a glass mountain where he found a golden bird, and a golden fish that danced to the sounds of a music tree.

A wild carp.

Today goldfish are popular pets. They are found throughout the world in aquariums and ponds. Scientists have found that goldfish can tell the difference between colors and shapes. They can learn to come to a whistle and take food from your hand. Goldfish are beautiful to watch, and are easy to keep. You can buy goldfish in pet stores, and ask store owners for advice on taking care of them.

These goldfish are going from pet store to a new home.

Goldfish: Inside and Out

How goldfish breathe underwater

Goldfish breathe oxygen just as you do. You get oxygen from the air. But oxygen is also carried in water, and fish take it from water by their gills.

Gills are inside the goldfish. They are behind its mouth, and hidden under bony plates called *gill covers.* Gills are thin tubes filled with blood. They resemble the teeth of a comb.

Goldfish suck in mouthfuls of water, and pass it over their gills. The oxygen goes into the blood through the gills, and the rest of the water flows out under the gill covers. The blood carries the oxygen to all parts of the goldfish's body.

How goldfish swim

Goldfish use their *fins* to swim forward or backward, to change directions, to stop, and to balance themselves in the water. Fins look like wings. They are part of the skin of the goldfish. Tiny bones hold them open.

Goldfish also use their bodies and tails to swim. When the goldfish wants to go forward, it moves its body and tail from side to side. The force of each movement pushes its body against the water, and sends the fish forward.

Slime, skin, and scales

The outside of the goldfish is covered with three layers — the slime, the skin, and the scales.

Slime is a thin coating, like a clear sticky jelly. Tiny holes are scattered throughout its surface.

Slime is a germ killer that heals wounds. And it keeps plants and animals that live in the water from attacking the skin. Slime also keeps too much water from passing into the fish's body. Otherwise, the goldfish's body would swell up with water, and stop working.

Beneath the slime is the goldfish's soft skin. Bony plates called *scales* are fastened into the skin. These scales cover the goldfish's body, except for its head. Overlapping one another like shingles on a roof, the scales protect the goldfish. And as the fish grows, each scale grows.

Some scales are so thin that you cannot see them. Goldfish with these scales are called "scaleless," even though they aren't.

One goldfish, called the pearl scale, has scales shaped like half-pearls.

Pearl Scale

Color

Underneath the scales are tiny cells of coloring matter — pigment — which give the goldfish most of its color.

A goldfish's pigments are orange, yellow, black, and violet. The bright blues, reds, and other colors you see in some goldfish are made by mixtures of these colors, and by the play of light on them.

The Goldfish's Underwater World

Goldfish can see, smell, taste, feel, and hear. If you suddenly move your hand toward goldfish, they dart away. If you drop food in the water, they swim toward you.

Eyes

In their underwater world, goldfish do not see things clearly. You can see the difference when you open your eyes underwater. Only the closest objects are sharp and clear. Everything else is out of focus or blurred.

The goldfish's round eye lenses let the fish see those objects closest to it. Faraway objects are blurred.

The eyes, however, do let the goldfish see light, colors, and shadows, in the water. But in deep waters where light fails to reach, goldfish cannot see.

Goldfish can see in more than one direction at

a time. This is because their eyes are on the sides of their heads, not in front. When the goldfish looks ahead, its two eyes work together, just as yours do. But, to see things on the left, it uses its left eye. To see things on the right, it uses its right eye. Sometimes, one eye can look ahead, while the other eye looks to the side.

Goldfish can see colors, and can tell the difference between shades of color. You can find out which color your goldfish likes best by doing the following experiment.

Place a piece of red paper under half of the goldfish bowl. Put a piece of blue paper under the other half. Make sure the lighting is the same on both sides. On which color does your goldfish rest? Try other colors. Does it make any difference?

Experimenting with light and dark papers under aquarium.

This koi is sleeping.

Eyelids

Goldfish sleep with their eyes open; they don't have eyelids. The water in which they live bathes and cleans their eyes.

Smelling and tasting

A goldfish usually finds its food by smelling and tasting the water. Inside its nose are special organs of smell.

Other organs, called *taste buds*, can taste food. You have taste buds, too, on your tongue. Taste buds are scattered on the goldfish's tongue, head, tail, and fins. So, the fish tastes its food even before taking it into its mouth.

You can watch your goldfish taste and smell the water. Pour a cupful of water in which another goldfish has been swimming into the aquarium. Watch what happens. Your goldfish may swim up to the water, nudge it, and try to find the fish that isn't there.

A calico pompon tasting water.

Hearing

You cannot see the goldfish's ears. They are inside its head.

Tiny bones connect its ears to the goldfish's swim bladder. Sounds coming into the swim bladder travel through these bones and go into the ears.

Feeling

The goldfish feels through nerve organs scattered over its skin. These organs are found mostly around the head and lips.

Through these nerve organs, the goldfish can feel temperature changes in the water. Its body temperature changes with the temperature of the water in which it is swimming. The goldfish has no control over its temperature. It is a cold-blooded animal like the snake.

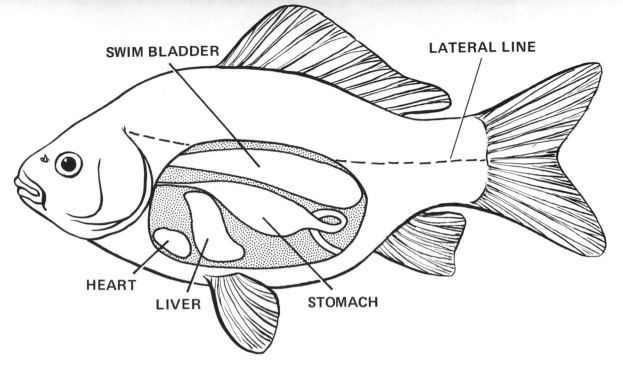

SWIM BLADDER

LATERAL LINE

HEART

LIVER

STOMACH

The swim bladder is connected to the goldfish's ears. It carries sounds. The swim bladder also helps the fish keep its balance by inflating in deep water and deflating in shallow water.

Lateral line

The goldfish has a line of sense organs on its body which help it feel. A goldfish can feel objects without being near them. It feels an insect dropping into the water. It feels a person walking along the bank of a pond. It feels objects moving around it, and senses which ones are food, and which ones are other goldfish.

A goldfish does all these things with its lateral line.

The lateral line looks like a broken line running down each side of the goldfish from its gill cover to its tail.

The broken line is really many openings in the skin. Inside these openings are special sense organs. Other openings, also filled with these sense organs, branch over the goldfish's head and face.

Scientists do not completely understand how the lateral line works.

Close-up showing lateral line.

All Kinds Of Goldfish

There are about 25 kinds of goldfish in the world. Most of the goldfish you see are the common and the comet goldfish. These fish are the easiest to keep at home. They are strong and healthy animals, and can live for 20 years or longer in an outdoor pond.

The Common Goldfish

Measured from the tip of its nose to the end of its body, the common goldfish may reach 24 inches (60 cm) in an outdoor pond. In a small aquarium, where there isn't much room to grow, the goldfish reaches only one or two inches (2.5-5 cm) in length.

It is usually gold or white.

Comet

Fish named for comets

The comet goldfish has a long, flowing tail which looks like the tail of a comet that rides the sky.

Propelled by its tail, the comet is the fastest swimmer of all goldfish. It makes a good pond fish because its swimming skills help it escape cats and other enemies lurking about the pond.

The comet may grow 20 inches (50 cm) long in an outdoor pond, and is usually red or gold in color.

Fish with a hat

Imagine a fish wearing a strawberry for a hat. This is what a lionhead looks like. The hat part is really a warty skin tumor. It grows thicker as the fish grows older. It may even grow over the fish's eyes and gills. Sometimes, the growth drops off by itself. If it doesn't, it must be cut off so the fish can see and breathe.

If the tumor becomes too heavy, the lionhead cannot swim. Struggling to keep its balance, the fish swims upside down. Sometimes, it hangs in the water with its head pulling it down like an anchor.

Most lionheads are orange with a red head.

Young lionhead. Arrow points to where its strawberry hat is just starting to grow. In a few years, this growth will be much larger.

Fish with peacock tails

The fins of the fringetail are always long. Its tail may be twice as long as its body. The fins of the veiltail and fantail are shorter. But, long or short, these fins form a gentle and graceful picture of color.

Fringetails, veiltails, and fantails are beautiful. Their long, forked tails fall into graceful folds like a peacock's tail. They are various colors of red, yellow, black, and blue. Sometimes they have colorful spots of purple, red, blue, yellow, or brown scattered over their bodies.

Watch a fringetail swim through the water. Its tail opens like an umbrella, and its back fin flows into waves.

Fantail

Fringetail

Moor Telescope

Fish with popeyes

There are goldfish with eyes that look like tiny telescopes poking out of their heads. These are telescope fish. Another name is "popeyes." These fish cannot see very well; some are blind.

One kind of telescope fish, called the moor telescope, is all black. When it grows older, it may turn red or gold.

Another kind of telescope fish is the celestial, meaning heavenly. Its eyes are tipped up, as if looking at the heavens. Celestials are poor swimmers. They can't see where they are going. They bump into other fish, and taste and smell everything in the aquarium until they finally stumble upon something to eat.

Celestial

Fish with whiskers

One relative of the goldfish has long, fleshy, growths called *barbels* on either side of its mouth. They look like whiskers.

These fish are koi (pronounced coy). *Koi* is the Japanese word for carp.

The koi's barbels are covered with taste buds. To find food, the fish runs its barbels over the bottom of the pond.

In Japan, koi are popular pets. The Japanese raise and sell these fish throughout the world. They even honor their sons on Boy's Day (a celebration like our Father's and Mother's Day) by flying paper koi on poles outside their homes.

The best koi cost from $10,000 to $40,000 each! But you can buy a pet koi for around $3.00.

You must keep koi in outdoor ponds. They need fresh water with plenty of oxygen, otherwise they become ill and die.

When fully grown, koi are about 16 inches (40 cm) long. They usually live 60 years or longer. A few have lived 200 years!

Koi like bread crumbs, and floating pellets that you can buy at pet stores.

You can easily train koi and other pond fish to take food from your hand. The best way to do this is to call them, and drop the food in the water. Do this for several days. Soon, the koi will swim to the surface for food when they hear you call.

Then put your hand filled with food on the surface of the water. Call the fish. Repeat this until the fish swim up to your hand. Lower your hand so the fish can reach the food.

Now wait until the koi swim up to your hand without calling them. Hold the food in your other hand and wait until the koi take it.

Feeding goldfish.

Homes For Your Goldfish

Setting up the aquarium

An aquarium, large jar, or bowl, make fine homes for goldfish. You should allow one gallon for each inch of fish. A ten-gallon (37 liters) aquarium, for example, is big enough for five goldfish that are two inches (5 cm) long. A goldfish is measured from the tip of its nose to the end of its body. You do not count the tail.

Before you buy an aquarium, however, think about the answers to the following questions:

How much money do you have to spend on an aquarium? How much money do you have for fish? Do you want small or large goldfish? How many goldfish do you want to keep? Do you want to breed the goldfish? How much money do you have for a heater or a filter or a pump?

Buy an aquarium that will suit your plans.

A jar or bowl is only good for one or two goldfish. Aquariums hold more.

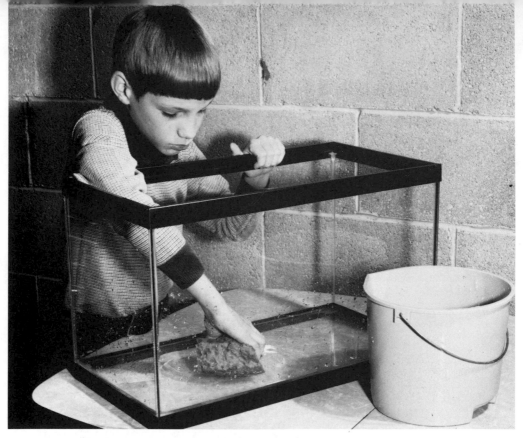

Washing out the aquarium with plain water — no soap!

The aquarium should be made of glass with a stainless steel frame, and a slate bottom. It should have a glass or stainless steel cover.

Place your aquarium in a shady spot where the sun never shines directly on it. Too much sunlight will cause the water to turn green with algae — scum.

When you are ready to set up your aquarium, wash it with cool tap water (water from the faucet). Never use soaps or cleaners!

Gravel

Cover the bottom of the bowl or aquarium with one or two inches (2.5-5 cm) of aquarium gravel which you can buy at pet stores.

Gravel about ¼ in. (6.4 mm) to ⅜ in. (9.6 mm) in size is best for goldfish. Rinse the gravel by placing it in a pan under running water. Put one (2.5 cm) or two (5 cm) inches of gravel on the bottom.

Plants

Plants are good in an aquarium but you can keep goldfish without them. If you want plants, place them in the gravel before you put the fish in the aquarium.

Among the best kinds of plants for goldfish are Vallisneria, Sagittaria, and Amazon swords. Cover the plant roots with gravel.

Then add aged water to within two inches (5 cm) of the top of the aquarium. Pour the water slowly so it does not disturb the plants.

Aged Water

Tap water contains chlorine and sometimes fluoride. These chemicals can kill goldfish. Chlorine and fluoride must be allowed to escape from the water before you put fish into it. This can be done by letting the water stand for 24 hours. This process is called *aging.* You can let water age in pans and clean plastic buckets.

You can also use a chlorine remover which quickly takes out chlorine from the water. Pet stores carry this product.

Aquarium plants: Vallisneria (eel grass) is on the left, Amazon swords in the middle, Sagittaria on the right. ➤

Water temperature

The best water temperatures for goldfish are from 55 to 70 degrees Fahrenheit (13 degrees C to 21 degrees C), about the same as room temperatures. So you do not need to have an aquarium heater.

However, sudden temperature changes shock goldfish. When you bring your fish home from the pet store, float the carrying bags in the aquarium for fifteen minutes. This allows the water in the bags to reach the temperature of the water in the aquarium.

Open the bags, and pour about ½ cup of water from the aquarium into each one. Keep the bags open. Slip the top of each bag under the aquarium cover to keep the bag upright. Do this five or six times every fifteen minutes, or until the bags are full of water. This gives the goldfish enough time to adjust to the chemicals and minerals in the aquarium water. Then slowly pour the goldfish and the water in the bag into the aquarium.

Floating the carrying bag in aquarium w

Lights

To grow plants, you need an aquarium light. Several kinds are sold in pet stores.

The light helps the plants make oxygen. The oxygen goes into the water, and the goldfish take it into their bodies. In turn, goldfish give out carbon dioxide from their bodies for the plants to use to grow.

The aquarium light should be left on four to six hours daily. Some plants, however, need eight to ten hours of light. Ask the salesperson where you buy the plants.

Bringing air into the aquarium

You may want a small electric air pump for your aquarium. Several kinds are sold in pet stores. The pump pushes bubbles of air through the water. These air bubbles bring oxygen into the tank, and carry away undesirable gases.

Filters

You can keep more goldfish in an aquarium with a filter than in an aquarium without one. Filters keep the water clean.

Charcoal and floss in the filter remove odors, discolored water, and undesirable gases. Pet stores sell water filters which can be used with pumps.

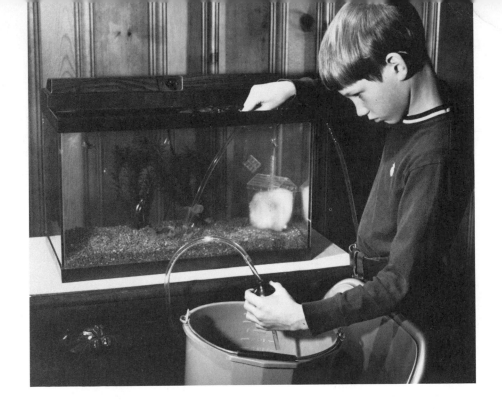

Taking care of the aquarium

It's a good idea to clean the aquarium once a week with a dip tube. The dip tube is a long rod which draws up waste materials from the top of the gravel.

If you don't have an air pump and water filter, remove half of the aquarium water every two weeks.

If you do have a pump and filter, remove ⅓ of the water once a month, and change the filter floss and charcoal.

One day before you remove the aquarium water, fill a clean plastic bucket with tap water and age it. The next day, remove the aquarium water. Replace it with the aged water from the bucket.

Pointers on Changing Aquarium Water

All the aquarium water should be changed at least once or twice a year.

Catch the goldfish in a net. Put the fish, and plants in a clean plastic bucket filled with aged water.

Remove all the aquarium water. Rinse the gravel under running water until the water runs clear. Scrub the filter, plastic tubes, and rocks with wire aquarium brushes. Change the floss and charcoal in the water filter. Wipe off the inside of the aquarium with paper towels.

Set up your aquarium again. Your goldfish will be healthier pets when you give them a clean home in which to live.

The pond aquarium

Another goldfish home can be made by filling an aquarium, or large jar, with water from a lake or pond. Keep it in a cool place, away from the heat, and out of direct sunlight.

Do not add food to the pond aquarium. The goldfish will eat *plankton* — tiny plants and animals living in the water. You need a microscope to see most plankton. Larger ones are easy to spot.

As the water evaporates, add more pond water so that the aquarium is always filled with water and plankton.

The outdoor pond

Almost all kinds of goldfish can be kept in outdoor ponds during the summer. In winter, however, only the hardiest ones survive. These include the comet, shubunkin, and common goldfish.

However, even for these hardy fish to survive the winter, a pond has to be more than three feet deep (0.9 m). Otherwise, the water may freeze all the way to the bottom.

When ice forms over the pond, don't break it to feed the fish. They don't need food. They will live off the fat of their bodies. In spring, they will be there to greet you.

Goldfish and tropical fish don't mix

Do not try to raise tropical fish with goldfish. Large goldfish may eat small tropical fish, and large tropical fish may nibble on goldfish fins. Furthermore, tropical fish need a high protein (meat) diet, and goldfish require a high vegetarian (plant) diet. Goldfish also need cooler water than tropical fish.

Minnows, however, can live with goldfish. You can catch minnows in lakes or ponds with a hand net.

Changes within your aquarium

You can learn much about underwater life by carefully watching what goes on inside your aquarium.

It's a good idea to keep records. Use a loose-leaf notebook or index cards to write down everything you observe.

There are many projects you can do.

You can, for instance, compare the growth rates of two plants or two goldfish. You can record the changes in the color of plants from season to season.

You can watch for bubbles on plants. These bubbles are oxygen being given off as the plants make food. Do you see more bubbles on sunny or cloudy days? Keep a record to find out.

Discover for yourself what temperature changes

Minnows live with goldfish.

occur in your aquarium. If you have two aquarium thermometers, place one in the aquarium, and one in a jar filled with tap water. Keep a room thermometer on a nearby table. Record all the readings on each thermometer every day for one week.

Then, compare the temperatures you have recorded. Compare the temperatures of the tap water to the temperatures in the room. This will help you find out if the glass of the jar affects the temperature of the water.

Now, compare the temperatures in the aquarium water to the temperatures in the jar of tap water. Both waters are in glass, so glass could not have caused any differences. The comparison, however, will help you discover if plants and fish can cause temperature changes.

Keeping Your Goldfish Healthy

Goldfish are hardy pets. If you keep the aquarium clean, goldfish will usually live for a long time. Illness is usually caused by poor living conditions, such as foul water produced by decaying food.

Goldfish swimming in foul water will come to the surface, and gulp down air. Drinking in an air bubble, the fish holds it in the back of its mouth near its moist gills. But, the gills cannot get enough oxygen from the bubble. Soon the fish will die.

Change the water — remember to age it — and give your goldfish the air its body needs.

Goldfish also need fresh clean water to drink. They swallow a little water with their food.

Buying a healthy goldfish

Before you buy a goldfish, look carefully at all its fins. The back fin should be upright and moving. A sick fish swims with its fins folded close to its

Selecting fish carefully is important.

body. Don't buy a fish with torn fins, missing scales, or bloody areas.

Look at the fish from the top. If its gill covers stick out at an angle, the fish is probably not well. Also check the other fish in the aquarium. If any look sick, choose your fish from another tank. One sick fish may make all the fish in a tank sick.

Feeding the right foods

The goldfish chews its food thoroughly. Its teeth are in its throat.

Goldfish like dried flake fish food and live foods, such as brine shrimp. If your pet store doesn't sell live foods, you can use small pieces of earthworms.

It takes only a few seconds to feed your fish daily. Give outdoor pond fish pellet food and bread crumbs. Give aquarium fish (unless they are in a pond aquarium) a pinch of food. If they eat all the food in five minutes, you are feeding the right amount. If they eat it all in less time, feed more. If you feed too much, extra food will sink to the bottom.

Goldfish cannot be left for more than a week without food. Pet stores carry vacation feeders, or blocks of food, that provide enough food for two weeks.

Treating a sick goldfish

You can tell if something is wrong with your goldfish. It may swim awkwardly and not eat. Its fins may be folded, or its skin may be covered with tiny white spots. See the spots on the fish below.

Putting triple sulfa tablets in the aquarium.

When you see a sick fish, it's best to treat all the fish in the aquarium. Use triple sulfa tablets, which pet stores carry. These tablets dissolve in water, spreading medicine throughout the aquarium.

Use an aquarium heater to keep the temperature of your aquarium about 70 degrees Fahrenheit (21 degrees C).

Feed the goldfish live foods, as they are easy to digest.

If your fish don't seem any better and you want to change brands of medicine, remove half of the water from the aquarium, and replace it with aged water. Then add the new medicine.

Fungus

One non-green plant, a fungus called *Saprolegnia*, is always present in aquarium water. However, the fungus attacks the goldfish only when it is injured, or in poor health. Appearing as white blotches, the fungus spreads quickly to all the fins until most of the body is covered, and the fish dies.

You can treat fungus with triple sulfa tablets.

Tail rot, fin rot

Tail rot and fin rot are caused by chilling, and poor feeding. The fish's tail or other fins rot away.

To treat these ailments, use triple sulfa tablets.

Wounds and cuts

Use triple sulfa tablets to treat wounds and cuts.

Parasites

Goldfish kept in outdoor ponds sometimes have parasites. These tiny creatures attach themselves beneath the fish's scales, and suck out the fish's blood and body fluids.

You can tell if your pond fish have parasites. The fish will rub themselves violently over rocks and against the sides of the pond, trying to get rid of them. Light green areas will appear on their skins, or white worms will stick out of their bodies.

Catch the infected fish in a hand net. Remove the parasites by putting tincture of iodine (sold in pharmacies) on the infected green areas. Never put the iodine around the gills, as it will flow into the fish's bloodstream and kill it.

If you can see white worms sticking out of the skin, remove them with tweezers. Paint these areas with the iodine.

Return the fish as quickly as possible to the pond. Treat the pond water with sulfa tablets.

How Goldfish Reproduce

Outdoors in the pond, the water gets warmer as the days grow longer in spring and summer. In the aquarium, a heater raises the water temperature.

When the water temperature and season are just right, the female goldfish's stomach swells. Her body has been making eggs for a long time. Now it is heavy, filled with from 500 to 2,000 eggs.

Within the body of the male goldfish, sperm (reproductive) cells develop. Tiny white dots pop out on each gill cover, and the body narrows near the tail.

These changes show you which sex your goldfish are. You cannot tell the difference until your goldfish are ready to breed. Goldfish will not breed until they are one year old. Then, they will continue to breed until they are six or seven years old.

The male goldfish is nudging the female across the water.

On a warm day, the female goldfish will lay her eggs. First, she swims for cover under leafy water plants. Two males follow. Nudging her stomach with their bodies, the males drive her back and forth across the water. With each nudge, the female releases small clusters of six to twelve eggs.

As the eggs fall, the males shed their sperm cells over them. The sperm flows into the egg cells and fertilizes them. You may see the eggs, like pale brown freckles, on plant leaves. Each egg is about this long - . It is covered with a sticky substance that clings to plants.

Eggs, greatly enlarged. You can see the fish growing inside.

Shubunkin resting on the bottom.

Spawning, or egg laying, usually begins in the morning, and lasts about three hours. After spawning, the goldfish sink to the bottom to rest.

Since goldfish eat any eggs that they find, you must remove either the fish, or the plants containing eggs to another aquarium or pond.

A goldfish hatches

From a shapeless mass, the baby goldfish begins to appear within the egg. You can watch the goldfish growing inside the egg. Look through a hand lens held close to the outside of the aquarium glass.

At first, the soft spine and color cells shine darkly through the egg. Then, two black eyes peer out at you. The egg begins to beat, as the heart pumps and the tail twitches.

On the fourth or fifth day, the egg shakes violently. Out pops a baby goldfish. It rushes for cover under a plant. Its mouth is like a suction cup, and clings to whatever touches it.

At this stage, the goldfish is called a *fry.* It is no longer than this —. Shaped like a thread, the fry is attached to an egg yolk sac. The sac contains food which the fry uses for the first two days after hatching. It gets all the food it needs from the yolk.

In two days, the fry is as long as this———. It begins to search for food.

Fry living in an outdoor pond will eat plankton.

In the aquarium, you must add food. You can use powdered baby egg-layer food from pet stores. Feed the fish this food for one week. Then, mix it with flake food. Crush the flake food with your fingers. In three weeks, your fish should be eating only flake food.

Your young goldfish will quickly become used to you. When you come to feed them, they will swim up to you. They can see your shadow through the glass, and hear you coming to the aquarium.

Glossary

AGING: letting tap water stand in a container for 24 hours

AIR PUMP: a small machine which pumps oxygen into aquarium water

ALGAE: tiny green plants (occasionally brown or red) living in aquarium water.

AQUARIUM: a water-filled container in which goldfish, other water animals, and sometimes plants are kept

BARBELS: long, fleshy growths on both sides of the mouths of some carp and koi

CARP: a brown and light-green freshwater fish that is used as food

CHLORINE: a chemical found in tap water and used to purify it

FINS: parts of the goldfish's skin which are held open by tiny bones

FRY: a young goldfish which has recently hatched from its egg

GILLS: hollow tubes filled with blood that take oxygen from the water

GILL COVER: a bony plate covering the gills

GOLDFISH: a colorful carp without barbels which is kept as a pet in home aquariums and outdoor ponds

GRAVEL: a mixture of pebbles and small rocks used to cover the bottom of an aquarium

KOI: a colorful carp which grows barbels, and is kept as a pet in outdoor ponds

LATERAL LINE: tiny openings in the skin of goldfish which run down each side of the fish from its gill cover to its tail

LENS: that part of the eye which does the focusing

OUTDOOR POND: a still body of water in which goldfish, other water animals, and plants may be kept

OXYGEN: that part of the air which goldfish and other animals breathe

PIGMENT: coloring matter found underneath the scales of goldfish

POND AQUARIUM: a container filled with water from a pond or lake in which goldfish, other water animals, and plants are kept

SCALES: bony plates which are anchored in the goldfish's skin

SLIME: a clear, sticky thin skin covering on the body of a goldfish

SPAWNING: laying eggs

TASTE BUDS: special organs on the goldfish's body which can taste food

TAP WATER: water from the faucet

TROPICAL FISH: small and colorful fish, native to the warm waters of tropical lands, which are kept as pets in home aquariums

WATER FILTER: aquarium equipment which contains charcoal and filter floss through which water passes in order to remove odors, discolored water, and certain gases

Index